EGYPTIAN WOODWORKING AND FURNITURE

Cover
Box, Eighteenth Dynasty, tomb of Perpaut, Thebes.
(Durham University Oriental Museum, 1460.
Photograph reproduced by courtesy of Durham University Oriental Museum.)

British Library Cataloguing in Publication Data
Killen, Geoffrey
Egyptian Woodworking and Furniture. –
(Shire Egyptology Series; No. 21)
I. Title. II. Series
749. 2932
ISBN 0-7478-0239-4

Published in 1994 by
SHIRE PUBLICATIONS LTD
Cromwell House, Church Street, Princes Risborough,
Buckinghamshire HP27 9AJ, UK.

Series Editor: Barbara Adams

ISBN 0 7478 0239 4.

First edition 1994.

Printed in Great Britain by
CIT Printing Services, Press Buildings,
Merlins Bridge, Haverfordwest, Dyfed SA61 1XF.

Contents

Acknowledgements

I would like to thank Barbara Adams, Editor of the Shire Egyptology series, and Jacqueline Fearn and John Rotheroe of Shire Publications for the help and guidance they have given me. I am very grateful to John Ruffle, Keeper of the Oriental Museum, University of Durham, for allowing me to examine both the Perpaut boxes preserved in that collection. I thank also Mr W. V. Davies, Keeper of Egyptian Antiquities at the British Museum, and his staff for their continued support and assistance. Most of this work was written in Cambridge and I would like to acknowledge the help given me by Barry Kemp, John Ray and the Librarian and staff of the Faculty of Oriental Studies. I am also indebted to Helen Whitehouse, Department of Antiquities, Ashmolean Museum, Oxford, for providing detailed information regarding fragments of furniture preserved in that collection. I am grateful, too, to the Director of the Egyptian Antiquities Museum, Cairo, Dr Ahmed Mohsen, for allowing me to research and study the wonderful collection of furniture preserved there. I would also like to thank my friends Robert Davies and Salima Ikram for suggesting a number of changes to the typescript. Finally I express sincere thanks to Lorraine March-Killen, my wife, for her continued support and in providing many of the splendid photographs which illustrate this book.

The outline dynastic chronology is based on that of Dr William J. Murnane and acknowledgement is made to him and Penguin Books for its use here.

4

List of illustrations

Chronology

Predynastic	5500 - 3200 BC	
	5500 - 4000 BC	Badarian
	4000 - 3500 BC	Naqada I (Amratian)
	3500 - 3300 BC	Naqada II (Early Gerzean)
	3300 - 3200 BC	Naqada II (Late Gerzean)
Protodynastic	3200 - 3050 BC	Naqada III (Late Gerzean)
Early Dynastic	3050 - 2686 BC	Dynasties I-II
Old Kingdom	2686 - 2181 BC	Dynasties III-VI
First Intermediate Period	2181 - 2040 BC	Dynasties VII-XI (1)
Middle Kingdom	2040 - 1782 BC	Dynasties XI (2) - XII
Second Intermediate Period	1782 - 1570 BC	Dynasties XIII-XVII
New Kingdom	1570 - 1070 BC	Dynasties XVIII-XX
Third Intermediate Period	1070 - 525 BC	Dynasties XXI-XXVI
Late Period	525 - 332 BC	Dynasties XXVII-XXXI
Graeco-Roman Period	332 BC - AD 323	*Alexander the Great* *Philip Arrhidaeus* Ptolemies Roman Emperors

1
Woodworking materials

A surprisingly complete record of carpentry in ancient Egypt can be pieced together through examining tomb scenes, archaeological excavations and discovered materials. From the earliest times basic ideas were turned into tangible products, setting the design principles that are still followed thousands of years later.

The properties of timber were understood and tools were developed to work it. At first these were basic hand tools, but then specialised tools and cutting aids were produced. Later, simple machine work increased output and enabled furniture to be provided for many homes. For example, by rotating the work in front of a stationary cutter, the lathe, a basic machine which has influenced many lives, was invented.

Sources of wood: native and imported

Large-scale timber production from indigenous trees was rare in Egypt. The scarcity of wood, which is generally poor in quality, created supply problems even during Predynastic times. It would have been possible only to convert wood into boards of short lengths with a small cross-sectional area.

The acacia was probably the most widely used of the native trees. Evidence of its use by woodworkers can be traced throughout the Dynastic Period. It was used not only in the making of furniture but also in boatbuilding and large constructional projects. A number of tomb and temple scenes showing the acacia survive. A piece of wood from W. M. Flinders Petrie's excavations at Kahun in 1895 is preserved in the museum of the Royal Botanic Gardens, Kew, where botanists have confirmed its identification as acacia.

The tamarisk was also available. It is a smaller tree and was probably not extensively used for timber production. This species has many defects such as knots and is usually found protecting desert villages from drifting and wind-blown sand. Willow, *Salix safsaf*, is also found in Egypt and was used in a limited way to make furniture. A fragment of a Ninth Dynasty coffin made from sidder, *Zizyphus spina-christi*, has also been identified at Kew, as have a number of pieces of sycamore fig, *Ficus sycomorus*, which date from the Eleventh Dynasty through to the Graeco-Roman Period.

With the problems of increasing demands for better-quality timber it is not surprising that the importing of wood began as early as the First Dynasty. The coast of the eastern Mediterranean proved to be the most popular source of Egyptian timber imports. As increased quantities of these new timbers reached Egypt during the Old Kingdom, the quality of woodworking improved.

Probably the earliest imported timber to be used was cedar, *Cedrus libani*. Large quantities were imported into Egypt from the Lebanon. The Palermo Stone, which records the royal annals of the early kings of Egypt, provides some important evidence of this. During the reign of the Fourth Dynasty Pharaoh Sneferu forty great ships sailed to the Syrian coast, where Egyptians felled trees and towed the logs back to Egypt. Egyptian carpenters and joiners exploited this excellent timber throughout the Dynastic Period: much of the funerary furniture discovered in the tomb of Tutankhamun was made from cedar.

Ash, *Fraxinus excelsior*, occurs naturally in North Africa and a beautiful compound bow discovered in the tomb of Tutankhamun was made from this wood. The shafts of axes and adzes were also carved from ash for it has tremendous elastic properties as well as being tough. The timber can also be bent artificially: in a scene from Beni Hasan, Middle Kingdom carpenters are shown steaming and bending wooden sticks (figure 1). The carpenter holds the wood over a pot of hot water, allowing the hot vapour to penetrate and soften the timber's cellular tissue. Another timber which can be steam-bent is elm, *Ulmus campestris*, and this would have been used by Egyptian wheelwrights during the New Kingdom.

1. Carpenters steam-bending lengths of timber, from the tomb of Baqt III, No. 15, Beni Hasan. (After Newberry, *Beni Hasan II*, London, 1893, plate VII.)

Oak, *Quercus cerris*, was also used and was probably imported from Turkey. Unfortunately it decays, unlike ebony, *Diospyros*, which is a black or dark brown wood of high durability with a very dense grain. Ebony would have been shipped from regions south of Egypt, such as Ethiopia. During the earliest dynasties only small supplies appear to have been available. However, in the tomb of Tutankhamun a splendid ebony bed-frame was discovered. A scene in the New Kingdom temple of Queen Hatshepsut at Deir el-Bahri shows Egyptians cutting branches from ebony trees in the land of Punt and African slaves carrying them to ships for transport back to Egypt. Ebony is very hard to work and furniture made from it was valued highly throughout the east Mediterranean region. Gifts of ebony furniture were made by the later kings of Egypt to the rulers of other countries.

Plywood

The technique of laminating thin sheets of timber, with the grain of one sheet being at right angles to the next, was known to Egyptian carpenters. An example of this early 'plywood' was discovered in a passage within the Step Pyramid complex of Djoser at Saqqara. This piece dates to the Third Dynasty and possibly forms part of the side panel of a coffin. It is an example of six-ply wood that is held together with wooden pegs. Egyptian carpenters obviously realised that this was a way in which they could produce a stable sheet of material with dimensions larger than the log from which it was fabricated.

Ivory

Ivory was used from as early as the Neolithic period, its close grain making it an ideal medium to carve. Many small legs of bovine shape, carved in hippopotamus ivory, have been discovered in the First Dynasty royal tombs at Abydos and at other Early Dynastic sites, such as Tarkhan. In the First Dynasty tomb of Djer many short legs, which were probably used to support small caskets, were found (figure 2). Preserved in the Fitzwilliam Museum, Cambridge, is a particularly fine example which is delicately carved with vein and tendon detail. There are examples

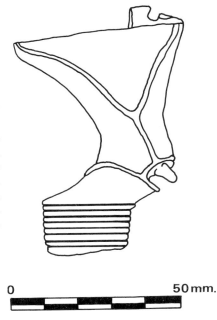

2. Ivory bovine-shaped leg which would have supported either a small casket or a stool; Tomb of Djer, Abydos, First Dynasty. (After Petrie, *The Royal Tombs of the Earliest Dynasties*, Part II, London, 1901, plate XXXIV[17].)

0   50 mm.

of such bulls' legs in museums around the world, notably in the Metropolitan Museum of Art, New York, although many are unprovenanced. Ivory from both the elephant and the hippopotamus was used to make a variety of artefacts and ceremonial objects.

Basket techniques

Basketwork too was practised from as early as Neolithic times. By plaiting natural fibres, such as the leaves of the date palm, some kinds of coarse grass and pliable plant stalks, craftsmen were able to weave many different types of basketware. The carpenters and joiners themselves used baskets of holdall type to carry their tools. It had to be reinforced with cord ribs and had a carrying handle (figure 3).

3. Carpenter's basket, Lahun, Twenty-second Dynasty. (Pitt Rivers Museum, Oxford, I 49. Photograph: Lorraine March-Killen.)

Reed and rush

Reed grows abundantly in the waters of the Nile and other marshy areas, such as the Delta, and was harvested to make simple boxes from Predynastic times. The hollow stems of this plant are rigid, making it unsuitable for basketry, but were an ideal material for the construction of wig boxes (figure 4). A framework of stout reed stems would have been bound together with rush or papyrus, with diagonal reeds often built into the framework structure to increase the box's rigidity. The side and base of the structure were faced with thinner reed stems, which were stitched in groups to the horizontal elements of the framework. The top edge of the box was often finished by covering the exposed and uneven stems with a strip of palm leaf, which again was bound into position with rush. The lid was of a similar construction and simply placed across the opening. A beautifully preserved wig box, now in the Egyptian Antiquities Museum, Cairo, was found in the Eighteenth Dynasty tomb of Yuya and Thuya at Thebes. Also rectangular in construction, it is designed with ventilation holes in the side walls. Other reed boxes were used to store food and, on occasion, writing materials and equipment.

4. Reed wig box, New Kingdom. (British Museum, London, 2561. Photograph: Lorraine March-Killen.)

Leather

Sheep, goats and cattle were domesticated and their skins used as clothing at an early date. Leather production was well established by the Predynastic Period. Tanning was achieved by treating skins with the juice from the fruit of the acacia tree. Leather was used during the Predynastic Period to make thongs for tying woodwork joints together, and the webbing of some early bed-frames and the seats of New Kingdom stools were formed from leather straps.

Upholstery

As well as straps made from leather, woven cord was used to make seats for chairs and stools. This is seen in the Second Dynasty stela of the Lady Heken at Helwan. On simple stools the cord was bound around the seat rails, while on more elaborate chairs holes were drilled through the seat rails and the cord was woven across to form the seat.

Cushions were used from as early as the Second Dynasty. A fine stela, from Saqqara, shows Sehefner seated on a low-back chair. The deceased sits on a cushion which is extended over the backrest of this chair (figure 5). The weaving of linen from flax was well understood by the beginning of the Dynastic Period. A linen cushion in the British Museum, thought to date from the New Kingdom, is stuffed with the feathers of waterfowl. Animal skins were also used as seat covers: leopardskin, imported into Egypt from Nubia and the Sudan, was highly favoured.

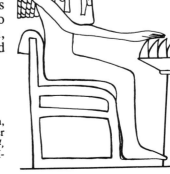

5. Stela showing Sehefner seated on a cushion, Saqqara, Tomb 2146E, Second Dynasty. (After Quibell, *Excavations at Saqqara 1912-1914, Archaic Mastabas*, Cairo, 1923, plates XXVI-XXVII.)

2
Woodworking techniques and fittings

Felling, timber conversion and fittings

The selection of wood for felling was an important process. Timber boards had to be cut from straight trunks of good quality which had sufficient heartwood with few defects. A fine illustration showing woodcutters felling a tree and feeding its foliage to three gazelles is seen in the Twelfth Dynasty tomb of Khnum-hotep III at Beni Hasan (figure 6). These men are using bronze axes which have a curved cutting edge with integral projecting side lugs. The blade fitted into a groove cut into the head of the ash shaft. Wet leather thongs were bound around the lugs and shaft and as they dried they pulled and tightened the assembly together.

After felling, the branches were chopped away and the trunk was cut into lengths of approximately 1.70 metres. This made the logs easy to transport and of the correct length to convert into boards. The logs were

6. Woodcutters felling a tree, from the tomb of Khnum-hotep III, Twelfth Dynasty, No. 3, Beni Hasan. (After Newberry, *Beni Hasan I*, London, 1893, plate XXIX.)

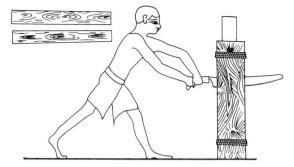

7. Carpenter working with a pullsaw, Eighteenth Dynasty. (After Davies, *The Tomb of Rekh-mi-re* at Thebes, New York, 1943, plate LV.)

brought to the courtyard of the carpenters' workshop. Set into the ground in the centre of the courtyard there would have been a sawing post, to which the log was lashed with cord. A carpenter would use a pullsaw to rip down the green timber. As the saw cut down the log, the lashings had to be adjusted (figure 7). Often a wedge or lever mechanism which operated with the aid of a heavy weight, perhaps a stone, was pushed into the top of the saw cut. This would help the saw to move freely through the wet timber. Ripping down timber by these methods is well illustrated throughout the Dynastic Period. We have no evidence to suggest that sawpits were used by Egyptian carpenters.

Trunks were always converted into boards by the 'through and through' process (figure 8). This minimised the amount of wastage but boards converted by this process were liable to cup, owing to tangential shrinkage (figure 9). The exposed slash-grain which results from using this conversion process (figures 7 and 10) can be seen when examining the timber.

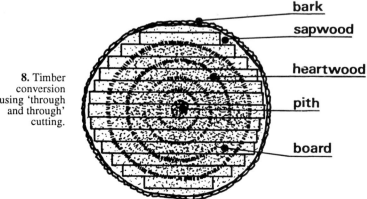

8. Timber conversion using 'through and through' cutting.

bark

sapwood

heartwood

pith

board

9. The cupping of timber caused by tangential shrinkage of boards cut by 'through and through' conversion.

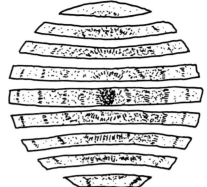

10. Typical slash-grain figure which is exhibited in timber converted by 'through and through' cutting.

Timber must be seasoned to make it easier to work. This also increases the timber's strength and helps prevent attack by fungi and some wood-boring insects. When felled, the wood's cell cavities and walls contain water, and this moisture content must be reduced to between 6 and 8 per cent. Egyptian carpenters were experienced in estimating the moisture content of timber. They realised that very dry atmospheric conditions would cause timber to dry out even further, resulting in additional splitting and shrinkage after it had been worked into its final form. Along the desert edge changes in atmospheric conditions are limited and this factor has helped to preserve large amounts of furniture.

The wet boards would have been rested against the walls of the workshop or stacked in wigwam fashion. It was important that air be allowed to circulate around the timber. The timber would not have been placed in direct sunlight and may have been covered with matting to prevent it from drying out too quickly in the hot dry Theban air, which would have seasoned it within a few months.

Joints

In many Predynastic burials the crouched body was placed in a simple box or on a frame of wood which had been covered with plant stems. Much of this early timber has decayed but from surviving pieces showing the corners and edges it is possible to identify a number of woodworking joints. The majority of boxes have butt-jointed corners held together with wooden pegs or tied with

11. Butt-joint.

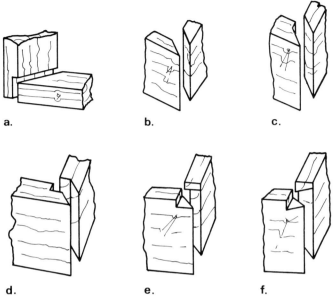

12. Box and frame corner joints: a, half-lap; b, simple mitre; c, shoulder-mitre; d, double shoulder-mitre; e, mitre-housing; f, dovetailed mitre-housing.

leather thongs which passed through holes in the joining members (figure 11). Other corner joints commonly used from the earliest times were the half-lap, simple mitre, shoulder-mitre, double shoulder-mitre, mitre-housing and the dovetailed mitre-housing (figure 12). Carpenters used the most complex of these joints on the largest of boxes as well as the smallest ivory jewel cases.

Carpenters and joiners were unable to use long lengths of timber for the length was determined by the height of the sawing post it was converted against. Longer rails were manufactured by scarf-jointing short rails together and locking them into position by using a butterfly cramp (figure 13). Unusually long solid pieces, used in major constructional works, were not converted by sawing but prepared directly from the log.

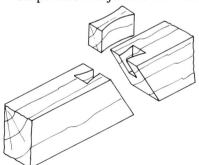

13. Scarf-joint with butterfly cramp.

14. Mortise and tenon joint.

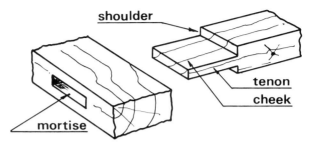

15. Dovetail joint.

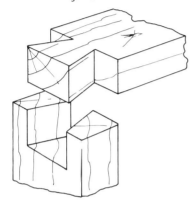

The bark and sapwood were removed by axe to expose the heartwood. The surfaces would then be trued with an adze, (figure 22), an ancient tool used very much like a modern plane.

The earliest extant mortise and tenon joint (figure 14) is seen in First Dynasty bed-frame construction, while dovetail joints (figure 15) are identified on the roof bars of a Fourth Dynasty bed-frame canopy which was discovered in the tomb of Queen Hetepheres at Giza.

Applied techniques

Gypsum, a hydrated form of calcium sulphate, occurs in Egypt in either rock or crystal form and was made into a thick plaster. It was applied to the surface of poor-quality timbers to disguise the grain and any exposed defects. If paint was to be used to decorate a piece of furniture, then a thinner ground made from whiting and gum or glue would have been laid on to the timber. This material is called gesso and made a perfect foundation for paint. The paints were made by finely grinding naturally occurring minerals and mixing the powder with water and an adhesive such as size.

Gilding was another technique applied to timber and was achieved by laying very thin gold leaf upon a wet film of gesso. This latter dried and acted as an adhesive holding the gold leaf firmly to the wooden core. Thicker gold foil, and sometimes silver, a metal not occurring naturally in Egypt, were pressed and punched on to the wooden core and held in position by small nails.

Veneers were also used to cover and disguise poor-quality timbers. Each leaf was cut with a fine-blade saw, unlike the modern technique of turning the log against a long knife. Ebony was extensively used as a veneer and was fixed into position with gum or glue and held with small dowels to prevent it from slipping or twisting while the adhesive set. Both ebony and ivory were used in sheet and strip form for inlaying into better-quality timbers. Other materials such as faience, which is a green or blue glazed non-clay ceramic (of crushed quartz, lime and natron), and polished stone, such as carnelian, were also inlaid into wooden furniture.

The ability of the carpenter to apply complex decoration is best seen with the techniques of marquetry and parquetry. Two boxes discovered in the tomb of Tutankhamun (Eighteenth Dynasty) have their panels decorated with thousands of tiny pieces of wood carefully arranged and glued into position in a herringbone pattern.

Clear varnish, made from resin mixed with oil, was used to protect timber during the Eighteenth Dynasty. Black varnish, made from pitch and oil, was also painted on wood to seal the grain. To cover and protect paintings, beeswax was often applied but it is uncertain whether it was used as a polish on timber, although it is the base from which many modern polishes are manufactured.

Decorative techniques

Furniture discovered in tombs was placed there for specific funerary purposes to accompany the deceased to the afterlife. Much was decorated with hieroglyphic symbols of religious significance to Egyptians (figure 16). Symbols such as the *was* (dominion), *ankh* (life), *neb* (all) and *djed* pillar (stability) were commonly cut from timber, gilded and then attached to the piece of furniture by pegs.

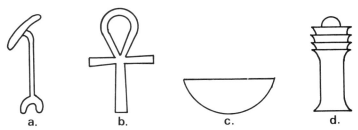

16. Hieroglyphic decoration applied to furniture: a, *was*; b, *ankh*; c, *neb*; d, *djed*.

Adhesives

The use of animal-based glues was not known until the Fifth Dynasty. The glue was made by boiling the skins and bones of animals in water and allowing the solution to evaporate, leaving a concentrated viscous adhesive. In an illustration in the tomb of Rekhmire at Thebes a carpenter

17. Carpenter applying hot glue with a brush to veneer, Eighteenth Dynasty. (After Davies, *The Tomb of Rekh-mi-re at Thebes*, New York, 1943, plate LV).

is applying hot glue from a stone vessel with a brush to a strip of veneer (figure 17).

Wooden dowels (and, in the Eighteenth Dynasty, large gold studs) were used to hold joints together as the glue was allowed to set. Nails and small tacks, cast from copper and precious metals, were also commonly used to hold various covering materials in place.

Fittings

Both wooden and gold butt-hinges were used on furniture. Barrel hinges made from interlocking cylindrical pieces of wood were also widely employed (figure 18). An extremely fine folding bed which uses a complex bronze hinging mechanism was discovered in the tomb of Tutankhamun. It is not unique, for a small model folding bed, dating from the New Kingdom, is preserved in the Metropolitan Museum of Art, New York.

Most boxes were secured by tying cord around a pair of mushroom-shaped handles set in the lid and front of the box. The cord would have been sealed with clay to provide rudimentary security. However, complex locks can be seen on better-quality boxes.

Sliding bolts running in metal staples or hoops were used to fasten together the hinged doors of boxes and cabinets from the Eighteenth Dynasty onwards.

18. Wooden hinge, Saqqara, Late Period, 547'69. (Photograph by courtesy of Birmingham Museums and Art Gallery.)

3
Predynastic and Early Dynastic Periods

Tools

Up to and during the Predynastic Period resistant materials were worked with knives and saws made from flint (figure 19) and simple copper tools were manufactured during the Badarian Period, 4500 to 4000 BC, to carve wood, ivory and stone. By the Naqada I Period (4000 to 3500 BC) basalt and other stone vases were being bored with copper drills and in Naqada II metal, stone and wood working proliferated. Therefore, by the beginning of the Early Dynastic Period and the unification of the lands of Upper and Lower Egypt into a single kingdom the technology was available to work wood and other materials with a high degree of accuracy. From then on the trades of craftsmen were regulated across the whole Egyptian state.

19. Flint saw, Badarian Period, *c.*4500 BC. (British Museum, 62274. Photograph: Lorraine March-Killen.)

The cut lines made from early copper saws can often be seen on planks of timber that were converted during the Early Dynastic Period. These run across the face of the timber in all directions, which indicates that the saw blades were short. The earliest examples of copper saws were discovered by Petrie at Abydos in 1899-1902 and 1921-2 and by Professor Walter B. Emery at Saqqara between the 1930s and 1950s. The series of mastabas Emery excavated included a burial chamber surrounded by a number of storerooms, which had contained many different funerary goods such as jewellery and household furniture.

Unfortunately the tombs had been robbed during antiquity and we have no idea of the material which was removed. What is more, the robbers started fires in each room, either maliciously or for the purpose of destroying evidence of their entry. The wooden roof appears to have extinguished the fire when it collapsed into the tomb. Much of the remaining wooden material was either smashed into fragments or reduced to charcoal.

One of the major discoveries Emery made was an enormous cache of saws and other woodworking tools in Tomb 3471. He dated them to the reign of Djer, who ruled during the First Dynasty. These saws were of

no value to the tomb robbers nor did they melt in the fire. The Early
Dynastic saws from Abydos and Saqqara were between 250 mm and
400 mm in length. The shape and profile are similar to many knives,
having slightly curved edges with a round blunt nose (figure 20). The
edges were beaten to increase the metal's hardness, at the same time
reducing the thickness of the edge. This leaves a slight rib along the
centre of the blade which extends into the tang that would have been
fixed in a wooden handle. The teeth, which start some way from the
shoulder of the blade and finish well before the rounded nose, are cut
along one edge. They are very irregular in shape and pitch, the gullets
being nibbled out, leaving the tip of many teeth flat. Since each tooth

20. Copper saw from the tomb of a courtier of Djer at Abydos, First Dynasty. (Courtesy of
the Petrie Museum of Egyptian Archaeology, University College London. UC. 16178.)

21. Ancient and modern saw sets.

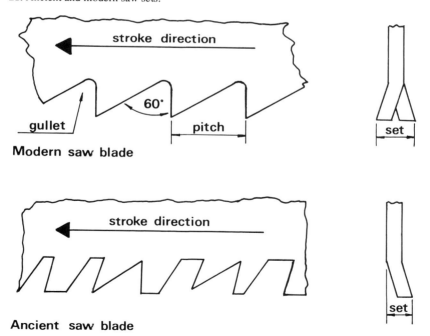

22. Adze, First Dynasty, Saqqara. (After Emery, *Great Tombs of the First Dynasty*, volume 1, Cairo, 1949, figure 19.)

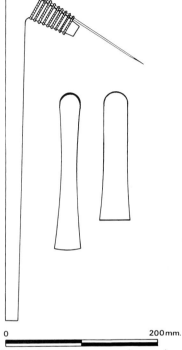

0   200mm.

was punched out from the same side, the 'set' of these ancient saws is unusual and not like the set of a modern rip-pattern saw, which provides a wide 'kerf' or saw cut (figure 21). When timber was being converted with these ancient saws, the kerf had to be wedged open to prevent the saw from jamming.

Also discovered by Emery were several straight wooden adze shafts and a large number of copper adze blades. The blades were cast in copper and then hammered into a flared shape before the cutting edge was ground on. On some blades both faces were ground with a cutting edge while on others the rake is found only on one side, like a modern plane iron. These blades were attached to their shafts with leather thongs, strips of linen or cord (figure 22).

Both mortise and firmer chisels were discovered in this cache of tools (figure 23). Those used for mortising were struck with wooden mallets and had large cylindrical handles with flat tops. The blades were square in section to prevent them from bending when chips of wood were prised out of deep mortises. The firmer chisel, by contrast, had a handle with a rounded top, which would fit comfortably into the palm of the carpenter's hand, suggesting it was used for handwork and carving. Its blade was rectangular in section and in general this tool was shorter in length than a mortise chisel.

Other copper tools discovered were thin-blade awls used to bore holes in timber and some small engraving tools.

Furniture

Many of the fragments of wooden furniture discovered in the First Dynasty tombs at Saqqara and Abydos are carved with a bound rush or 'basketwork' decoration. An assembled piece made from two fragments discovered separately by Émile Amélineau and Petrie in the tomb of Semerkhet at Abydos would have formed part of a box (figure 24). One

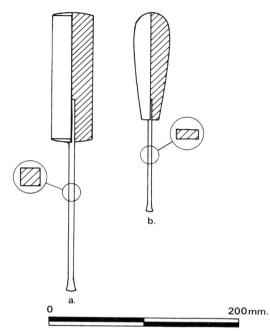

23. Mortise and firmer chisels, First Dynasty, Saqqara. (After Emery, *Great Tombs of the First Dynasty*, Volume 1, Cairo, 1949, figure 22.)

b.

a.

0   200 mm.

side has been bordered with a delicately carved bound rush pattern. This has been overlaid with fine linen which was used as a ground for gold leaf. Many small fragments of gold can still be seen in the incisions between the basketwork border and the plain panel below. In the centre of this is a *serekh* gateway, on which is seated the falcon god Horus. The reverse side is edged with a carved band of bound rush, which also was gilded. The main body is inlaid with small triangles of wood and moulded faience which have badly faded in colour. They were arranged in an alternating pattern and held in position with some type of yellow binding medium.

Ivory strips, which have been engraved with various straight-line, nail-head and interlocking chain patterns, were also used to decorate furniture (figure 25). They were held in position with small ivory dowels. These features have been discovered at both Saqqara and Abydos which suggests that carpenters were following common design practices in both Upper and Lower Egypt.

The best collection of Early Dynastic furniture was discovered at Tarkhan by Petrie. He found a number of bed-frames, which can be classified into five constructional types. The first, and most primitive, was made from four branches of timber which conveniently had right-

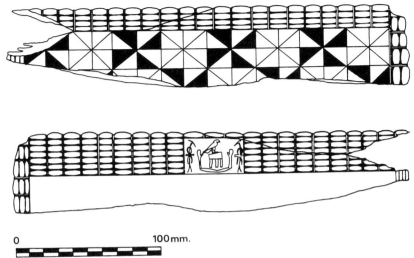

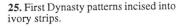

0   100 mm.

24. Furniture fragment with bound rush decoration, First Dynasty, Abydos. (Ashmolean Museum, Oxford, E1255 and E138.)

angled elbows formed in them (figure 26, bottom right). At the elbow of each was housed, in a round hole, the long straight end of the opposing branch. The short ends below each elbow formed the legs of the bed.

Also found at Tarkhan were rectangular bed-frames made from square-section timber rails that are supported on short square pillar legs (figure 26, top left). The frame is mortised and tenoned together, as are the legs, into the bottom surface of the long side rails (figure 27). This view shows that slots, through which webbing made from woven cord would have passed, were chopped at right angles through the bottom and inner surfaces of the side and cross rails.

The remaining three bed-frame constructions show that the frames were supported on bovine-shaped legs. The side and cross rails of the third and fourth types of bed-frame were made from poles. This required the curved shoulders of the tenons on the leg and

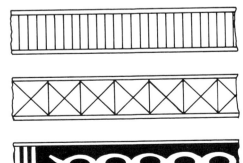

25. First Dynasty patterns incised into ivory strips.

those at the ends of the cross rails to be scribed to locate accurately against the side poles of the bed-frame. The legs are very finely carved and the hoofs may have been protected by encasing them in copper drums. Each leg was attached to the side rail by bindings made of

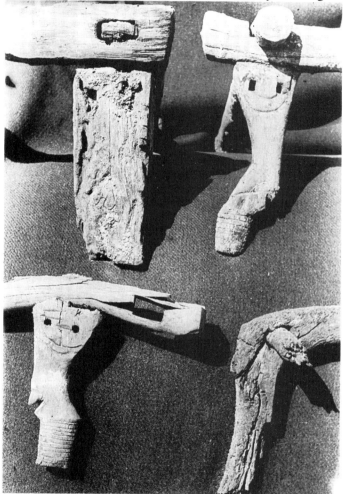

26. Bed-frame construction, First Dynasty, Tarkhan: (top left) pillar leg; (top right) bovine-shaped leg with cross rail above; (bottom left) bovine-shaped leg with cross rail mortised into side rail; (bottom right) primitive bed made from angled branches. (Archive excavation photograph, courtesy of the Petrie Museum of Egyptian Archaeology, University College London.)

27. Rectangular bed-frame, First Dynasty, Tarkhan. (Ashmolean Museum, Oxford, 1912.617. Photograph: Lorraine March-Killen.)

leather, which would have been soaked in water and then allowed to dry, so pulling the joint firmly together. Some of the better-quality bed-frames have slots cut into them to accept a wide cord webbing while others simply had the cord webbing woven around the poles of the frame. On one type, the leg, side and cross rail all meet in a common mortise (figure 26, top right). In the other type the cross-rail tenon is spaced away from the leg, leaving the leg to be separately mortised into the underside of the side rail (figure 26, bottom left). A fine example of this type of construction is preserved in the Manchester Museum (figure 28). It is 1.76 metres long and was the largest of the bed-frames discovered by Petrie at Tarkhan (though still smaller than the bed-frames commonly used today) and was converted from a short log. The ends of the side rails have handles carved in the shape of the papyrus flower, a common design feature found on furniture of this period and the Old Kingdom. The handles were also covered with leather sheet, perhaps glued into position with some primitive adhesive or shrunk into place.

28. Bed-frame with bovine-shaped legs, First Dynasty, Tarkhan. (Manchester Museum, 5429. Archive excavation photograph, courtesy of the Petrie Museum of Egyptian Archaeology, University College London.)

The fifth type of bed-frame discovered at Tarkhan and other sites in Egypt represents the best of the designs and the most complex to manufacture (figure 29). Like previous examples, it stands on short bovine-shaped legs which are mortised and tenoned into curved and

29. Bed-frame with curved side rails, First Dynasty, Gebelein. (Oriental Institute, University of Chicago, 12169. Photograph by courtesy of the Oriental Institute of the University of Chicago.)

moulded side rails. The cross rails are stub-mortised and tenoned into the side rails and webbing slots are chopped into the frame. The accurate shaping of the frame with its graceful curves illustrates the high degree of carpentry skills being practised by Early Dynastic craftsmen in a limited number of specially commissioned works. The joint of the leg and side rail is lashed together with a sophisticated binding of leather which also passed through slots in the cross rail. Only one end of the side rails has been carved with a stylised papyrus-flower handle. A similar bed-frame can be seen in the Musées Royaux d'Art et d'Histoire, Brussels.

Further interesting discoveries were made at Tarkhan. Two small tables were found, each of which was cut from a single block of wood. One was set on four projecting pads and the other on a pair of supports (figure 30). Petrie also discovered two sandal trays, again cut from solid blocks of timber and with a central bar of wood. This is shaped to the outline of a foot and the tray is hollowed out below (figure 31). This bar may have been used as a carrying handle, although the small projection at one end was perhaps intended for this purpose. Whether the tray was used to clean sandals or to hold some early chiropody implements or materials used in the cosmetic care of feet we do not know.

30. Low table, First Dynasty, Tarkhan. (The Manchester Museum, University of Manchester, 5456. Photograph: Lorraine March-Killen.)

We have no conclusive evidence of chairs or stools being used as funerary furniture in these First Dynasty tombs at Tarkhan, Abydos and

31. Sandal tray, First Dynasty, Tarkhan. (Ashmolean Museum, Oxford, 1912.606. Photograph: Lorraine March-Killen.)

Saqqara. The first examples of seats are depicted on a number of stelae discovered in the Second Dynasty tombs at Helwan by the Egyptian Egyptologist Zaky Y. Saad in 1952. From these we can establish that stools, with bovine-shaped legs of similar construction to the bed-frames, were commonly used by Egyptians during the Second Dynasty. One stela from Helwan shows Nefer-meri-ka seated on a stool with the ends of each side rail finished with a papyrus-flower terminal. The stela has been carved in an unusual way to show both the side of the seat and its top in one view (figure 32). Another stela, of Prince Nisu-heqet, is remarkable, for it shows him seated on a chair with a high back post and a stretcher below the seat (figure 33). Being of royal descent, the prince would normally be expected to be portrayed seated on a special piece of furniture and so it seems reasonable to assume that this might represent an early throne.

32. *Left:* Stela of Nefer-meri-ka, Second Dynasty, Helwan, Tomb 246 H8. (After Saad, *Ceiling Stelae in Second Dynasty Tombs*, Cairo, 1957, figure 9.)

33. *Right:* Stela of Prince Nisu-heqet, Second Dynasty, Helwan, Tomb 946 H8. (After Saad, *Ceiling Stelae in Second Dynasty Tombs*, Cairo, 1957, figure 4.)

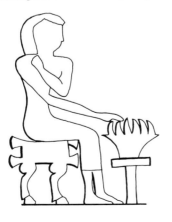

4
Old Kingdom

Reliefs and wall paintings

The few bed-frames and illustrations of early seats discovered in tombs of the Early Dynastic Period indicate the kind of furniture commonly used then. All of these pieces of furniture would probably have been found in the houses of both middle and high ranking officials and their families.

By the Third Dynasty, which marks the beginning of the Old Kingdom, major advances in building construction and the associated trades of woodworking and furniture manufacture are seen. The improvement in the design of furniture can be seen in a series of remarkable wall paintings in the Third Dynasty mastaba of Hesire at Saqqara. Hesire was chief of dentists and physicians during the reign of Djoser, whose Step Pyramid can also be found at Saqqara.

One of the earliest scholars to excavate sites in Egypt was the Frenchman Auguste Mariette. He opened the tomb of Hesire during the mid nineteenth century and discovered eleven wooden panels, five of which are displayed in the Egyptian Antiquities Museum in Cairo. Each had been beautifully and precisely carved in raised relief to portray Hesire in a number of elegant positions. One shows him seated on a typical animal-leg stool whose side poles are finished with papyrus-flower terminals.

After these panels were removed from the mastaba its position was forgotten and it became hidden under the moving Saqqara sands. The tomb was reopened in 1911 by J. E. Quibell, who discovered the furniture paintings which Mariette had overlooked. These paintings show a complete set of typical furniture which would have been used to furnish homes of the Old Kingdom and they show how design and technical developments in furniture production had advanced since the previous era. The quality of the furniture displayed indicates the use of imported timbers; furthermore, emphasis on applied and decorative techniques is beginning to be an established rule.

The bed-frames and stools illustrated in the tomb paintings are generally similar to those already described. The patterns rendered on these pieces of furniture suggest they were made of, or veneered with, timbers such as ebony. Two types of bed-frame are displayed, one with bovine-shaped legs and the other in an unconventional form with curved or bent elements which are set on a drum (figure 34). Both types slope slightly towards the foot of the bed, where a separate frame is placed to stop the bedding from slipping off. Again stools and chairs are to be

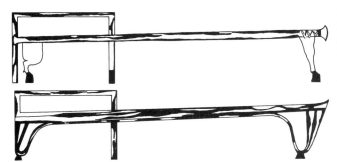

34. Two bed-
frames, Third
Dynasty, tomb of
Hesire, Saqqara.
(After Quibell,
*The Tomb of
Hesy*, Cairo,
1913, plate XX.)

found in the traditional bovine form. However, there were also a pair of rectangular stools and a chair with a framework back rest which have curved supports below their seats (figure 35).

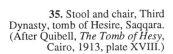

35. Stool and chair, Third
Dynasty, tomb of Hesire, Saqqara.
(After Quibell, *The Tomb of Hesy*,
Cairo, 1913, plate XVIII.)

The most interesting pieces of furniture in these tomb paintings are four splendid chests (figure 36). Each is of a framework construction fitted with wooden panels. The interiors would have been divided into compartments that would have held jewellery. Between the centre and bottom rails is set a decorative pattern of hieroglyphic symbols which appear to be either gilded or carved in ebony. Similar chests were found in the New Kingdom tomb of Tutankhamun.

36. Two
boxes, Third
Dynasty, tomb
of Hesire,
Saqqara.
(After Quibell,
*The Tomb of
Hesy*, Cairo,
1913, plates
XVII and
XVIII.)

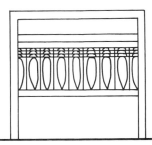

The furniture of Queen Hetepheres

In 1925 George Reisner, an American Egyptologist, discovered the furniture of Queen Hetepheres at the bottom of a deep shaft close to her son Khufu's pyramid at Giza. Her body was not found in this small chamber, leading Reisner to believe that the tomb where she had originally lain had been robbed and her body stolen shortly after her death. The contents of that tomb were moved to this second chamber, which would have been under tighter security, being within the Great Pyramid complex.

Queen Hetepheres was the wife of Sneferu, and in this small chamber Reisner discovered a complete collection of Fourth Dynasty royal furniture. Much of it had been encased in gold sheet and parts were inlaid with faience. When Reisner opened the chamber he found that much of the wooden furniture had rotted away, leaving only powder with the gold sheet and inlay scattered across the tomb floor. From the position of these remains he and his assistants were able to reconstruct much of the queen's furniture. This took many years of patient industry and as the work progressed copies were made that are now exhibited

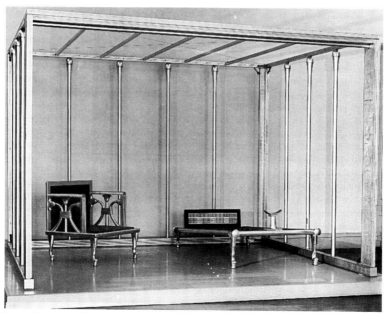

37. Reproductions of Queen Hetepheres' canopy and furniture, Fourth Dynasty, Giza. (Museum of Fine Arts, Boston: canopy 38.873, chair 38.957, bed 29.1858. Photograph: Departmental Appropriation, May 1938. Courtesy Museum of Fine Arts, Boston.)

both in the Egyptian Antiquities Museum in Cairo and the Museum of Fine Arts in Boston.

The queen's furniture would have been placed within a canopy made from wooden jambs, battens and poles that were finely gilded (figure 37). The entrance jambs have inscriptions raised in relief which give the name and titles of her husband, Sneferu. The back pillars, which are carved with a matted pattern, are held together with copper staples. The floor and top rails are fixed to the vertical corner posts with a number of complex joints, and poles are spaced around the walls of the frame. Roof poles have also been dovetail-jointed into the top rails of this canopy.

To prevent wear at the joints, each has been carefully encased with copper plates that have been folded to shape and tacked through the gold sheet to the wooden core below. This suggests that the canopy was portable. Around the walls and across the roof were hung, on copper hooks, netting and curtains which provided the queen with privacy and protection from insects and comfort from the chilling night air.

Two armchairs had been placed in the tomb, but unfortunately only one could be reconstructed. Each had legs of lion form and stood on copper drums and shoes. The back support of the reconstructed armchair shows that it was made from a mitred frame that was covered in gold and enclosed a plain, solid-wood panel. The chair's arms were semi circular in section and the vertical front posts were raised with a matted pattern. The spaces below the arms were filled with a spray of three tied papyrus flowers, carved in the round and covered with gold sheet. A cushion may have been placed on the wooden seat, which was made from another solid panel.

Also discovered was the queen's bed, which again was covered in gold sheet and stood on lion legs. The general shape is similar to those beds discovered in the Early Dynastic Period but it slopes, like the Hesire illustrations, downwards towards the bed's foot. Boards have been rebated into the side poles of the bed, on which the queen would have slept. For the first time a footboard has been attached to the bed. It was inlaid with many pieces of coloured faience in a feathered pattern, which is also repeated on a long box which held the curtains that hung around the canopy. Two smaller boxes were also found that contained the queen's bracelets and a headrest.

In the tomb of Queen Meresankh III at Giza are scenes showing servants making a bed under a similar canopy (figure 38). Queen Meresankh III was the wife of the Fourth Dynasty King Khaefre and her furniture rivals that of Queen Hetepheres in the quality of its design. Her armchair had panels filled with a seated lion and the bed is again similar to that of Hetepheres. The bed appears to have a mattress and the servants are arranging the bed clothes, with one positioning a simple

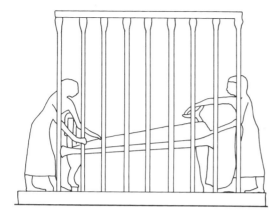

38. Bed canopy, Fourth Dynasty, tomb of Queen Meresankh III, Giza. (After Dunham, *The Mastaba of Queen Mersyankh III*, Boston, 1974, figure 8.)

headrest at the top of the bed. Also discovered in the tomb of Queen Hetepheres was a carrying chair, a similar one to which is shown in relief in the tomb of Queen Meresankh III (figure 39). These carrying chairs are of frame and panel construction and are attached to a pair of long poles which have handles of papyrus-flower shape.

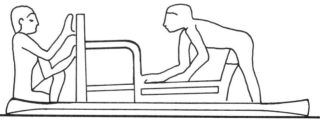

39. Carrying chair, Fourth Dynasty, tomb of Queen Meresankh III, Giza. (After Dunham, *The Mastaba of Queen Mersyankh III*, Boston, 1974, figure 5.)

Headrests

Another headrest is placed on a box below Queen Meresankh's armchair. Egyptians did not use pillows. Instead they used a wooden support to rest their heads on. Generally, headrests have a solid base and a carved head support which were connected by a short tapered column which was mortised and tenoned at both ends. Egyptian women shaved their heads to help with personal hygiene and wore wigs that were stored in reed boxes. Using a headrest might appear to us uncomfortable: some were padded inside but the majority were not. Possibly they were customised to fit an individual's head. Many examples of these headrests are displayed in museums. Most are of a simple construction such as those illustrated in the tomb of Queen Meresankh III. Some were produced with fluted columns and a few are elaborately decorated or covered in gilt like that of Queen Hetepheres. They also occur in stone, alabaster and in amuletic form.

Egyptians would have slept on their side when using a headrest and in Kenya and other parts of Africa they are still used today.

Tools

One of the most important mastabas at Saqqara, is that of Ti, which dates to the Fifth Dynasty. The walls of his tomb are carved with many reliefs showing scenes of activities performed as part of the normal daily life. One scene shows a number of carpenters manufacturing boxes and a bed under which is a headrest of the fluted column type. One pair of carpenters are hand-finishing the lid of a long box which is similar to the curtain box discovered in the tomb of Queen Hetepheres (figure 40). They are using sandstone blocks to smooth the grain of the timber, rubbing the block with the grain and not across it, which would have scuffed and damaged the timber surface.

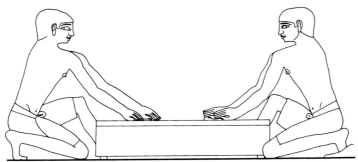

40. Wall relief showing carpenters sanding a box, Fifth Dynasty, tomb of Ti, Saqqara. (After Wild, *Le Tombeau de Ti*, Cairo, 1966, plate CLXXIV.)

Another carpenter is using a bow-drill to make a handle hole in the lid of a simple rectangular box (figure 41). He kneels in front of the box he is working on, his right hand holding a bow. A length of cord is attached to both ends of the bow and is wrapped with a single turn around the wooden stock of the drill. His left hand applies pressure to the copper drill bit through a stone cup which fits over the top of the wooden drill stock. As the bow is pulled back and forth it rotates the drill stock and a hole is drilled by the copper bit.

Above the carpenter can be seen an adze and saw. The shape of the saw had been modified by the time of the Fifth Dynasty. It has a distinct straight back with the teeth set along a curved cutting edge. The handle

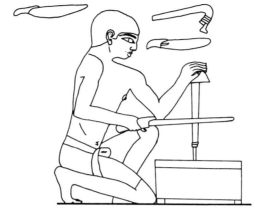

41. Carpenter using a bow-drill, Fifth Dynasty, tomb of Ti, Saqqara. (After Wild, *Le Tombeau de Ti*, Cairo, 1966, plate CLXXIV.)

has been moulded to fit the carpenter's hand, to give a more comfortable grip.

Early boxes

The origins of the bed-frame, stool and chair were firmly established by the end of the Early Dynastic Period. It was during the Old Kingdom that boxes developed in all shapes and sizes. In the Old Kingdom tombs at Saqqara there are many wall reliefs which illustrate this. Earlier boxes were made from plain boards that were corner-jointed together while later examples are of frame and panel construction. Some are painted while others are inlaid or veneered. In the Fourth Dynasty tomb of Queen Meresankh III a number of simple rectangular boxes are illustrated, some having round or barrel-shaped lids (figure 42). By the

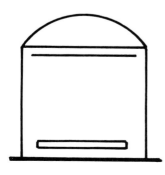

42. Box with round or barrel-shaped lid, Fourth Dynasty, tomb of Queen Meresankh III, Giza. (After Dunham, *The Mastaba of Queen Mersyankh III*, Boston, 1974, figure 5.)

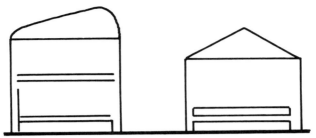

43. Two boxes, Sixth Dynasty, burial chamber of Penu, M.VII, Saqqara. (After Jequier, *Tombeaux de Particuliers, Contemporains de Pepi II*, Cairo, 1929, figure 50.)

end of the Sixth Dynasty lids are shown in both the shrine and gable form (figure 43).

Egyptians used boxes to carry heavy loads over long distances. An early illustration in the tomb of Queen Meresankh III shows a plain rectangular box carried on a pair of poles by two porters (figure 44). The box appears simply to rest on the carrying poles. The improvement in the quality and design of these larger boxes can be seen in the Sixth Dynasty tomb of Mereruka (figure 45). This box is of frame and panel construction with a gable lid set on a cavetto-shaped cornice with a torus moulding below. The carrying handles are separate elements and can be pushed in under the box when not being carried. The handles, which run in copper staples, would have been shaped so they could not be fully withdrawn. An almost identical box was discovered by Howard Carter in the tomb of Tutankhamun in 1922.

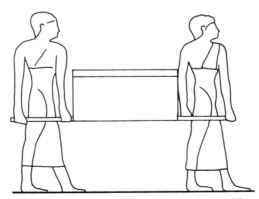

44. Porters carrying a box on a pair of poles, Fourth Dynasty, tomb of Queen Meresankh III, Giza. (After Dunham, *The Mastaba of Queen Mersyankh III*, Boston, 1974, figure 8.)

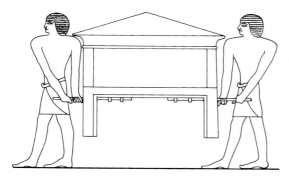

45. Porters carrying a large chest, Sixth Dynasty, tomb of Mereruka, Saqqara. (After Duell, *The Mastaba of Mereruka*, Chicago, 1938, plate 69.)

Mouldings

The first example of a cavetto cornice can be found on a pavilion in the *heb-sed* festival courtyard within the Third Dynasty Step Pyramid funerary complex of Djoser at Saqqara. A torus moulding was also applied to the sarcophagus of King Menkaure, who ruled during the Fourth Dynasty, and was discovered at Giza. This sarcophagus was unfortunately lost at sea while being transported to London in 1838. From as early as the Fifth Dynasty mouldings were decoratively applied to boxes. A particularly fine example is illustrated in the tomb of Ti. The curved surface of the cornice has been vertically ribbed, perhaps with plaster, and then gilded.

5
Middle Kingdom

Furniture

The Middle Kingdom necropolis of Beni Hasan is situated on the east bank of the Nile between Cairo and Luxor. Cut into the limestone cliffs, which overlook the Nile, are a number of Eleventh and Twelfth Dynasty tombs. These tombs were built for the nomarchs of the Sixteenth Nome, or administrative district, of Upper Egypt. These powerful men ruled almost independently of the king. One of their duties was to regulate work produced in state or temple workshops, and scenes in their tombs show carpenters at work.

Private individuals could have furniture commissioned only through the patronage of the nome. This tight supervision of work was necessary to conserve those raw materials which were available. Each workshop had an inspector, who received instructions from an overseer. He was probably a dependant of the nomarch.

On a slight slope below these nomarchs' tombs was an immense burial ground where the small tombs of those civil servants, officials and dependants who served the nome were sited. These people were buried in some splendour in small burial chambers which were discovered at the bottom of a deep pit. Their tombs were excavated by John Garstang, Professor of Archaeology at Liverpool University, during the 1902-4 seasons. He cleared 880 small tombs, the contents of which have now been widely dispersed. Some pieces remain in public collections while others are privately owned.

In tomb 569 Garstang discovered a stool whose legs are shaped in a typical Middle Kingdom style (figure 46). Each leg is tapered to a small

46. Stool, Twelfth Dynasty, Beni Hasan. (Ashmolean Museum, Oxford, E.4162. Photograph: Lorraine March-Killen.)

47. Seated ergonome on a Middle Kingdom seat.

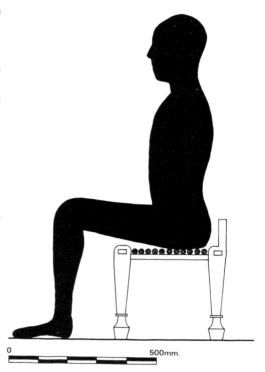

waistband from where the foot curves sharply and is set on a bevelled shoe. The top of each leg is rounded, with a pair of crossing through-mortises below. The end of each seat rail is cut with a common tenon that has two shoulders. To strengthen the frame, wedges would have been driven into the cheeks of each joint. The long edges of the seat rails are also rounded to prevent wear to the reed seat.

The most important burial to be discovered was tomb 183, which was attributed by John Garstang to Dedyt-baqt. He found in this tomb a table, the legs of two seats and a headrest. The table was edged with a cavetto cornice and was set on a sturdy under frame. The shapes of the seat legs are again typical of a Middle Kingdom style, with the rear legs having a short back post.

Three similar legs, from Beni Hasan, are preserved in the museum of the School of Archaeology and Oriental Studies, University of Liverpool. Unfortunately the back and seat rails have been lost. With measurements taken from the stool in tomb 569 and from the three legs in Liverpool, it has been possible to draw a scaled diagram of this seat (figure 47).

These Middle Kingdom seats were smaller than chairs used today. The living stature of a well-built Egyptian male of this period was 1.70 metres, about 40 mm shorter than the average modern European male. Both the tibia and femur were smaller and the hip height less. This was reflected in the seat height, which is the most important measurement when designing a chair. It is curious that Egyptian carpenters used the lowest possible seat height when making chairs. Perhaps they were governed by the social class of its intended owner or there was pressure on them to conserve timber. However, a lower seat height does give a more comfortable sitting posture. The legs can be extended in front of the body and the soft sensitive tissue behind the knees does not come into contact with the seat.

Because of the crossing mortise joints in the legs the seat rails are not in the same plane. The seat, which was made from bundles of reed stems bound together with five strands of cord, would have been placed on the lower side seat rails. This mat made a solid block which under load compressed and gave adequate support.

Important directional changes in Middle Kingdom furniture design can be studied by examining the furniture illustrated on stelae from that period, especially the large collection housed in the Egyptian Antiquities Museum, Cairo.

These Middle Kingdom stelae show that tables were widely used for displaying vases or holding water pots. They are usually very low, with either straight or splayed legs and with a single stretcher strung below the table top (figure 48a). A particularly fine splayed-legged table with cavetto cornice and double stretcher (figure 48b) is similar to the table discovered in tomb 183 at Beni Hasan.

Stools rarely appear in these stelae, for the majority of seats are designed with a short back support over which is draped a cover or cushion. They have either straight legs or plain legs fashioned in the

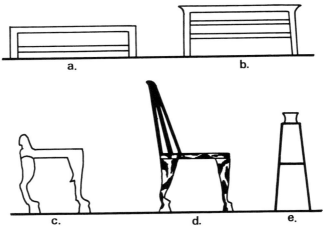

48. Middle Kingdom furniture illustrated on stelae in the collection of the Egyptian Antiquities Museum, Cairo: a, table, General Catalogue 20756; b, table, General Catalogue 20561; c, stool, General Catalogue 20010; d, chair, General Catalogue 20232; e, vase stand, General Catalogue 20755.

form of the front and hind legs of a bull or lion (figure 48c). Also illustrated are a small number of elegant chairs, some having slender, gazelle-shaped legs. An interesting example shows that chairs are given complex curved back supports, of full height, made from angled slats of timber. They are jointed into the rear seat rail and into the underside of a curved and moulded top rail (figure 48d). The surface of the chair illustrated in the stela simulates animal skin. Perhaps chairs would have been veneered or painted to create this effect. In the Egyptian Antiquities Museum, Cairo, are preserved a painted shield and arrow quiver case which resemble cowskin and date from this period.

Slender vase stands supporting single vases are also to be found in this collection. The tops are fitted with a moulded cup of wood into which the round or tapered bottoms of vases or bowls could be seated (figure 48e).

Tools

In 1888 Petrie discovered a Middle Kingdom workmen's town at Kahun. These craftsmen worked in the temple workshops built by Sesostris II and lived close by, within a walled enclosure. The town's architect had set out rows of terraced houses of about 50 metres in length, each branching at right angles from the enclosure wall and separated by a street. These parallel streets joined a central avenue which led to the temple complex and its workshops.

Each house had a wooden door that was set within an arched brick entrance. The pivots on the edges of the doors were set into holes in the floor and the arch above the door. These dwellings had a number of small rooms, some of which were covered with a barrel vault while others were spanned with large wooden beams which were covered with thatch. Some roof spans had to be supported with wooden pillars.

The setting out of the house rows was very precise and the shape and size of rooms were strictly controlled. The walls were plastered with daub and painted yellow. Some were decorated with paintings – one depicted a wooden vase stand, an early example of *trompe-l'oeil.*

Beneath the floors of these houses were found the poignant remains of babies who had been buried in small rectangular boxes by their parents. Such boxes would also have been used, more mundanely, to hold tools and other domestic items and were made from planks of timber fixed together with dovetailed mitre-housing joints (figure 49).

Furniture made of wood and even sometimes stone was commonly used in these houses. Petrie discovered an animal-leg chair with a slanting back support which was held to the side seat rail with an angled bracket fixed with small dowels.

The tools used by the carpenters who lived in the town were discovered

49. Wooden box, from the workmen's village of Kahun, Twelfth Dynasty. (Pitt Rivers Museum, Oxford, L48. Photograph: Lorraine March-Killen.)

within the temple complex. In a small hole a number of chisels and an adze blade were found. Petrie also discovered many other metal carpentry tools on the Kahun site. These tools were made from bronze, an alloy of copper and tin. This technological advance in tool manufacture is first identified in Egypt during the Middle Kingdom. Perhaps bronze was imported from Syria in ingot form during this period. Again the quality of carpentry improved as this new material was used. Blades made from bronze are harder, and therefore retain their cutting edge longer, than copper tools.

Toilet boxes

During the Middle Kingdom boxes were customised and used for special purposes. One interesting type contained eight small alabaster vases which held perfumes and oils. A tray cut with holes was placed inside a simple rectangular box to prevent the vases from moving and being damaged. The tray often fitted tightly and finger holes or a slot were cut through the centre of the tray to help with its removal.

A beautiful toilet box was also discovered here at Kahun by Petrie. It had belonged to a daughter of Sesostris II, Princess Sit-Hathor-Yunet, whose tomb, which was close to her father's pyramid, contained jewellery and a number of boxes. These boxes had decayed, leaving only the ivory inlays and the applied decoration of gold Hathor heads, carnelian and faience. Two boxes were successfully reconstructed by the conservation department of the Metropolitan Museum of Art, New York, where they are now displayed. Both have shrine-shaped lids, while one has been divided into compartments to hold the princess's toilet equipment. This consisted of a polished metal mirror, cosmetic containers, a silver rouge dish and a razor and whetstone.

Scribes' boxes

Scribes also used wooden boxes to store their pens and writing material. They were often left plain, or they were painted to suggest cedar panels, with ivory and ebony inlay.

6
New Kingdom

Tools

New Kingdom carpenters had an extensive tool kit and equipment to draw upon (figure 50). They used axes, large and small adzes, pullsaws and handsaws, bow-drills, mortise and firmer chisels, mallets and awls.

Egyptian carpenters, like their modern counterparts, used a hone to sharpen the cutting edge of their tools. It was made from slate and usually had a hole bored at one end which allowed it to be hung on a peg somewhere in the workshop. The centre of the hone would become dished by the repeated honing action. Many marks can be seen along such hones while a few run across them, these marks being made by the carpenter when, after sharpening the blade, he turned it over on to its flat side to wipe away the burr (figure 50).

To assist in the honing of blades a small amount of oil was applied to the surface of the stone. The oil would be held in a hollow horn, which was capped at one end with a round wooden stopper while at the other

50. Bronze woodworking tools, New Kingdom, Thebes. (British Museum, London, 6037, 6040, 6042, 6043, 6044, 6046, 6055, 6061, 22834, 30083, 30245, 36728. Photograph reproduced by courtesy of the Trustees of the British Museum.)

was a wooden spout formed in the shape of a spoon. A length of cord would have been attached to both ends of the oil flask, allowing it to be hung up, perhaps with the hone (figure 50).

The straight edge, used to test that the timber was true, was also part of a carpenter's equipment. The New Kingdom carpenter in figure 51 is preparing and squaring lengths of seasoned timber. He sits on a dished stone seat and works at a wooden bench. This is made from a log that has been specially worked and rebated across the front to help him saw lengths of timber. He has safely placed his adze in the top of the bench to protect his fingers and feet from the cutting blade. Also shown is a try square, the stock and blade of which would have been made from wood. To help him cut angles on timber, he had a mitre-cutting aid, which is shown behind the bench.

51. Carpenter using a straight edge, try and mitre squares. (After Davies, *The Tomb of Rekh-mi-re at Thebes*, New York, 1943, plate LV.)

Furniture

Stools would have been the most widely used pieces of household furniture. Egyptians used a number of different types of stool and the quality depended upon the rank of its owner. The lattice stool was probably the most popular with all classes of Egyptians and is widely illustrated in Theban tomb scenes.

The construction of the stool is very elegant, having four slender legs into which are jointed at the bottom a cross rail and at the top a curved seat rail. The space below the seat on all four sides was filled with vertical struts and angled braces. Some of these are tenoned into mortises in the horizontal elements while others are simply wedged into position (figure 52). The seat is always formed with a double cove construction of curved wooden slats or woven cord which pass through holes in the edge of the seat frame.

Round-legged stools were also used and are displayed in some of the more important Theban tombs. The legs were hand-carved and then finished by sandstoning. They were not turned on a primitive lathe. Examination of the many fragments of round legs reveals the irregularity

of the handwork and the absence of scraping marks which would be expected if the piece were turned. Also the shoulders of the legs are not square and there is no pivot hole in the bottom of the leg.

A fine example of this type of stool is preserved in the British Museum, London (figure 53). The incised bands and lines around each leg are very uneven and imprecise. The top of each leg is inlaid with small pieces of ivory in lotus-petal and droplet shapes. The ebony stretchers are tenoned into blind mortises in each leg. A simple ivory plaque bordered with ebony indicates where the mortise would have come through. Ivory ferrules, shaped in the form of a papyrus flower, are attached to the end of each stretcher and are moulded to fit against the leg. Ivory braces and struts are placed below the seat and are used solely to embellish the stool and are not part of the load-bearing construction. Each of the seat rails was heavily plastered before a sheet of leather was laid over the wet plaster to form the seat. Unfortunately this seat has decayed but fragments of it can still be seen attached to the seat rails.

53. Round-legged stool, New Kingdom, Thebes. (British Museum, London, 2472. Photograph: Lorraine March-Killen.)

Before the New Kingdom, carpenters either squatted or sat cross-legged on the workshop floor. This is seen in a model of a carpenters' workshop that was discovered in the Eleventh Dynasty tomb of Meket-Re at Thebes. However, New Kingdom wall paintings at Thebes show us that carpenters often sat on three-legged stools: a pair of these workmen's stools were discovered in the Nineteenth Dynasty village cemetery at Deir el-Medina.

The seats of these stools were each made from a thick slab of timber which was carved to a dish shape. Three curved legs were jointed at angles into the underside of the seat. Occasionally the leg tenon would pass through the seat and in these circumstances the surface of the seat was heavily plastered to conceal the mortises and also the poor-quality timber from which it was often manufactured. The seats of some stools were made from the end offcuts of unwanted logs. Several defects such

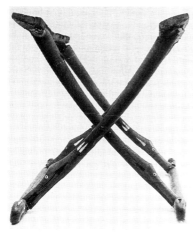

55. Folding stool, New Kingdom, Thebes. (British Museum, London, 29284. Photograph: Lorraine March-Killen.)

56. Chair, New Kingdom, Thebes. (British Museum, London, 2479. Photograph: Lorraine March-Killen.)

as heart and radial shakes would develop in the seat and were again covered and filled with plaster (figure 54).

The folding stool first appeared in the Middle Kingdom although the best examples come from the New Kingdom. It was designed for ease of transport, being light and convenient to handle when folded. When unfolded, the frame proves to be very rigid. Middle Kingdom folding stools were made simply from two interlocking frames held together with a pair of bronze pivots. Those from the New Kingdom are more elaborate, the vertical spindles often being finished with goose heads that are inlaid with ivory neck feathers and eyes. The beak of the goose formed the scribed shoulders of the tenon. This tenon projected as the goose's tongue and was mortised into the floor rail. Both floor rails are also carved with goose-headed terminals which are inlaid with ivory eyes (figure 55).

A leather seat was fixed to both of the curved seat rails with animal glue, which has darkened with age to a brown crystalline substance. Some seats were made from cord which passes through holes along the edge of the seat rails and is then woven across to form a wide flexible webbing. Although designed to be folded, some stools were made with solid wooden seats, shaped and painted to simulate an animal skin. A number of these stools are illustrated in Theban tombs of this period and a fine example was discovered in the tomb of Tutankhamun.

Chairs would have been found only in the homes of the wealthy middle class. Many are decorated with hieroglyphs and those with straight-panelled backrests were inlaid with ivory and ebony motifs. These chairs have short, lion-shaped legs which are set on small copper drums.

Egyptians also used a plain utilitarian chair with straight, square-sectioned legs and a curved backrest (figure 56). The front pair of legs are rounded at the top while the back legs are extended to form a tapered back post. Both the front and back pairs of legs are braced with stretchers and the seat rails all lie in the same horizontal plane. This is achieved by using half-width tenons, a technique not practised until the New Kingdom. Although animal glue was available it appears that carpenters still preferred to wedge these joints.

The back posts are jointed to a curved and moulded top back rail which is braced further with a central vertical support. Two angled back-support braces run from the ends of the moulded top back rail to be jointed into both side seat rails. Within the enclosed space are set a curved bar and four inclined struts which form the backrest.

The seat, like many other New Kingdom chairs, is made from a precise rush weave which passes through holes bored along the inside edge of the seat frame.

Vases and pots were still held in slender stands that were made from thin strips of timber which were mortised, tenoned and dowelled together

57. Vase stand, New Kingdom, Thebes. (British Museum, London, 2470. Photograph: Lorraine March-Killen.)

(figure 57). The table of this stand has a hollow centre with a thick wooden collar which prevented the bottom of round or tapered vases from toppling over. The frame was lightly gessoed and then painted with light green, dark green and red rectangles.

Apart from stools, chairs and vase stands, the homes of important officials also contained beds, tables and storage chests. A marvellous collection of private furniture was discovered in 1906 by Ernesto Schiaparelli in the Eighteenth Dynasty tomb of Kha at Deir el-Medina. Kha was an architect and belonged to the rich middle classes. His home would have been elaborately decorated and comfortably furnished. The range of furniture discovered in his tomb clearly illustrates the degree of affluence such high-ranking officials enjoyed.

His furniture, which comprises 32 pieces, is now displayed in the Museo Egizio, Turin. All of the four classes of stool discussed earlier were deposited in the tomb, together with the master's chair. Two simple rectangular wooden tables with square legs and horizontal stretchers were also discovered. They were gessoed and had bands of hieroglyphs painted across their tops. Other interesting pieces of furniture discovered in the tomb were a small table made from short poles, which gave it a rustic appearance, and two reed tables and a reed stand, all constructed in a lattice style and bound together with rush and grass.

The beds of Kha and Meryt, his wife, were like others of this period. They have long curved side rails which are supported on lion-shaped legs. The footboard was made from three panels separated by a pair of spindles. It was attached to the bed by large right-angled braces which were dowelled to each edge of the footboard and the top surface of the side rails. The weight of a sleeping person would make the bed's cord webbing droop in the middle. The braces across the long side rails are therefore curved to prevent the body coming into contact with them. This design feature is common to all New Kingdom beds.

The bed clothes and linen were stored in five painted gable-lid chests. Two were painted entirely with geometric patterns in green, yellow, black and red. The other chests each have a painted scene on one side that shows the couple receiving offerings of food.

Boxes

Two boxes of similar design to the Kha chests are now preserved in the Oriental Museum, University of Durham. They come from the tomb of Perpaut, which was probably excavated during the early nineteenth century by adventurers, who sold the contents of such tombs to private European collectors.

The construction and decoration of these indicates that Perpaut was a contemporary of Kha. Another box in Bologna, together with a round-legged stool in Leiden and a three-legged table preserved in the British Museum, London, can all certainly be attributed to Perpaut. Most probably a large number of other uninscribed objects in both public and private collections originate from this Eighteenth Dynasty Theban tomb.

The lid of the largest box is closed by sliding it into position along a pair of runners. A latch would then swing down from inside the lid and lock it. The shape of the grooves and runners ensured that the lid could not be lifted off and a backstop on the end of the lid stopped it from being pushed off its runners. This ingenious locking system could be overcome by forcing the box open. This indeed happened after its discovery but we may assume that it contained only bedding and linen (figure 58).

The lid is painted with a typical geometric pattern that is also used to decorate large areas of tomb walls of the period. Both long sides have painted scenes showing Perpaut accepting offerings made by his son and daughters. The ends are painted with scenes of rearing gazelles feeding from an ornamental tree. This design is first seen in a wall painting in the Middle Kingdom tomb of the nomarch Amenemhat at Beni Hasan.

The sides and ends are made from solid boards which butt against the rebated legs. The legs are painted with black lozenges upon a gesso foundation. Each of the scenes painted on side and end panels is framed with black and white lines which suggest stringing of ebony and ivory.

The second box is of poorer quality and again has a gable-shaped lid. This box gives side access, which is made by opening one leaf of the lid

58. Box, Eighteenth Dynasty, tomb of Perpaut, Thebes. (Durham University Oriental Museum, 1460. Photograph: Lorraine March-Killen.)

59. Box, Eighteenth Dynasty, tomb of Perpaut, Thebes. (Durham University Oriental Museum, 1459. Photograph: Lorraine March-Killen.)

(figure 59). Two mushroom-shaped handles are set into the centre of the lid on each side of the ridge. No sophisticated locking system was used on this box: the lid was simply tied down by winding cord around both handles and then sealing the cord together with clay.

The construction of this box is quite rough and ready and large amounts of plaster were used to conceal its faults. The panels were painted in an ochre colour and were framed with black and white lines. The legs and edges of the gable lid are again painted with a black lozenge pattern ruled between black lines and set on a white background.

In the tomb of Any at Thebes a toilet box which belonged to his wife, Tutu, was discovered (figure 60). This fine box exhibits precise cabinet-making skills, being of a frame and panel construction with the joints glued together. The interior has been divided into four compartments which held Tutu's toilet equipment and cosmetics. Placed in each of three small compartments at the rear of the box were vases which contained perfumed oil. The long front compartment held a bronze cosmetic-mixing dish and the lady's gazelle-skin slippers. Other items commonly placed in these boxes were polished bronze mirrors, kohl containers (for eye makeup) and ivory combs.

Below the base of the box is a decorative lattice of round dowels. The foot of each leg is rounded and was probably originally encased in a bronze protective shoe. The lid is held in position by a pair of tongues projecting from under the back of the lid. These located in notches cut into the back rail of the box. The front was held down by tying papyrus

60. Toilet box of the lady Tutu, New Kingdom, tomb of Any, Thebes. (British Museum, London, 24708. Photograph: Lorraine March-Killen.)

strands around a pair of mushroom-shaped handles and sealing the cord together with clay.

Theban tomb wall paintings also show that these smaller boxes were carried by porters under a pole. Lengths of cord were tied to copper hoops which were fastened into the front and back faces of the box. The centre of each length of cord was then placed over a long pole which was lifted and carried on the shoulders of two porters. Two porters could carry three suspended boxes by this method.

Jewellery boxes

Jewellery of this period was stored in small, highly ornate boxes. Usually the box carcase would be made from solid cedar boards that were simply butt-jointed together. The surface of the box was then applied with strips of ebony, which gave the appearance that it was made from a frame of rich dark timber (figure 61). The edges were disguised with small pieces of ebony and ivory laid alternately along each seam. The imitation panels are veneered with a central slab of red-stained ivory which is framed by two bands of ebony and ivory stringing. Between these are glued small squares of faience and ivory separated by thin strips of the stringing materials.

The lid of this box is decorated with veneered material in a similar fashion to the sides. The handles, which are set into the front of the box

61. Jewellery box, New Kingdom, Thebes. (British Museum, London, 5897. Photograph: Lorraine March-Killen.)

and lid, are carved from ivory in the traditional mushroom shape.

Royal collections

The splendid collection of furniture discovered in the tomb of Tutankhamun in the Valley of the Kings at Thebes is typical of palace furniture of that period. These illustrious examples, however, are not very different in style from those used by the middle classes. However, the quality of the woodwork and its embellishment are often quite exceptional. Royal furniture would have been covered in gold sheet, inlaid with coloured glasses or faience, veneered with rare timbers, exquisitely painted or decorated with royal symbols like the uraeus.

Unfortunately no other royal tomb has been found intact at Thebes although we do have a pair of armchair panels from the throne of Tuthmosis IV, now in the Metropolitan Museum of Art, New York. Also preserved are fragments of a chair of state in the Dundee Museum and Art Gallery and the footboard and legs of a bed-frame which belonged to Queen Hatshepsut, now in the British Museum, London.

Another collection of royal furniture was discovered by Theodore Davis in the tomb of Yuya and Thuya at Thebes in 1905. This couple's daughter, Tiye, married Amenophis III and he presented them with two magnificent chests. One of these chests has a round lid covered with gilded hieroglyphs and cartouches which bear his name. Also placed in the tomb were two armchairs made for Princess Sitamun, the couple's granddaughter. Again their quality indicates the exquisite craftsmanship of the royal workshops at the Theban necropolis.

7
Late and Roman Periods

Little furniture has survived from these later periods. During the Third Intermediate Period the administrative capital of Egypt moved to Tanis in the Delta, where the royal tombs of the kings of the Twenty-first and Twenty-second Dynasties were located. These small tombs were discovered virtually intact by Pierre Montet in 1939. They contained no furniture and their wall scenes are mainly funerary in subject matter; they do not show the everyday activities performed as part of normal life that are seen in earlier tombs.

An exception to this general rule is to be found in the tomb of Petosiris at Tuna el-Gebel, which dates to the regency of Philip Arrhidaeus, 323-305 BC, in the Graeco-Roman Period. Here the fine series of tomb reliefs have been freed from religious content. These scenes show furniture similar to that of previous dynasties, with the addition of a folding table, on which a carpenter works with a bow-drill, and a type of lattice or wicker chair.

The most interesting scene in Petosiris' tomb shows a pair of carpenters using a primitive vertical lathe (figure 62). Set into the ground is a pillar, which is also used as the tool rest. The turned leg is supported on pivots between the top and bottom stocks. These seem to have been adjustable and were probably wedged into place to accommodate the different lengths of timber which would be turned. One man rotates the wooden element with a length of rope while the other is scraping the wood away. Egyptian turners used flat-blade scrapers and angled skew

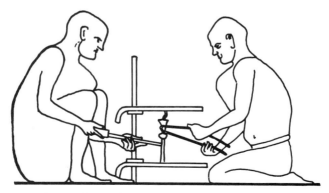

62. Carpenters turning wood on a simple lathe. (After Lefebvre, *Le Tombeau de Petosiris*, Cairo, 1923, plate X.)

63. Turned couch leg, Late Period or Roman Period. (Wellcome Museum, University College of Swansea, W 2061. Photograph: Roger Davies; reproduced by courtesy of the Wellcome Museum, University College, Swansea.)

chisels. No evidence has been found to suggest they used hollowed blade gouges.

Turned material soon became widely used to make the legs of chairs, stools and beds. At first the technique proved difficult on the light lathe illustrated in the tomb of Petosiris. Soon heavier and more rigid lathes allowed turners to produce quality material in a large number of complex profiles (figure 63).

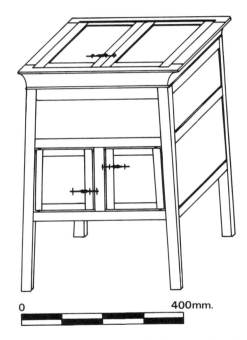

64. Cabinet, Late Period. (Louvre Museum, Paris, E 2773.)

0   400mm.

Cabinet-makers at this time were producing quality chests (figure 64). Designed upon a splayed frame with rebated panels, they had pairs of opening front and lid doors.

By the Roman Period, Egyptian homes would have been furnished with a number of pieces of quality furniture. Tables, stools and benches would have been a common feature. However, the couch, which was fashioned with turned legs and was finely upholstered, was also used in Egypt. Many examples of turned couch leg (figure 63) survive in museums around the world. These couches would have been inlaid with ivory and bone which were carved with scenes of animals, fruits and flowers. Some fine examples of bone inlay strip, from Tanis, are preserved in the Bolton Museum and Art Gallery. Marble was often used to make furniture or the tops of tables, while bronze was cast and made into vase stands. In the Musée des Beaux-Arts, Lyons, is a particularly fine three-legged bronze vase stand which was found near Alexandria in 1773.

It was during the Roman Period that carpenters first began using planes and worked on timber prepared over a sawpit. By converting timber in this way it became possible for carpenters to work on boards of better quality and longer length. The art of the woodworker, joiner, cabinet-maker and turner, founded in antiquity, has been continually practised through fifty centuries. From master to apprentice, these ancient skills and techniques are preserved and cherished.

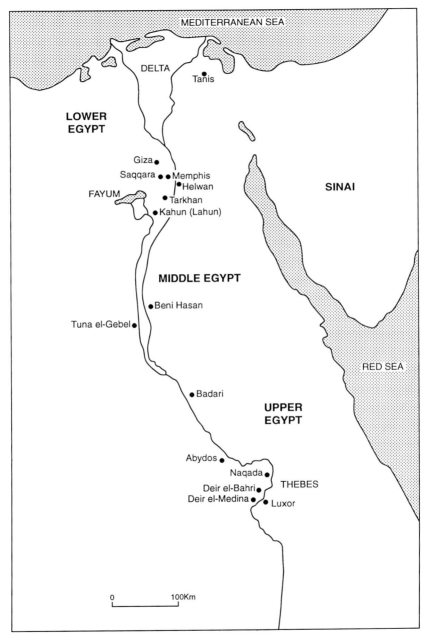

MEDITERRANEAN SEA

DELTA

Tanis

LOWER
EGYPT

SINAI

Giza

Saqqara ● ● Memphis
● Helwan

FAYUM

● Tarkhan

● Kahun (Lahun)

MIDDLE EGYPT

● Beni Hasan

Tuna el-Gebel ●

● Badari

UPPER
EGYPT

RED SEA

Abydos ●

Naqada ●

Deir el-Bahri ●   THEBES
Deir el-Medina ●
● Luxor

0   100Km

65. Map of Egypt, showing sites mentioned in the text. (Cartography by Robert Dizon.)

8
Glossary

Cheeks: the exposed and cut faces of a joint.

Double cove seat: seat that has four curved seat rails.

Green timber: wet and unseasoned wood.

Heartwood: the heartwood lies under the sapwood and its cells are hard and do not contain sap. It is usually stable and less likely to decay and is used for furniture construction.

Sapwood: the sapwood surrounds the heartwood and its cells transport water and minerals from the ground to the branches and leaves.

Sawpit: a deep pit over which is placed a framework of wood which supports a timber log, which is sawn, with a long two-handled saw by two men. One man stands in the pit and the other above on the framework.

Shakes: if the timber is felled or seasoned incorrectly then defects such as shakes develop. These are splits which open into holes across or along the grain.

Slash sawing: the log is sawn into boards along its axis. This conversion process is also known as through and through cutting.

Tangential shrinkage: when a log is slash-sawn it is cut at a tangent to the growth rings. Cupping or deformation of the board occurs because it does not dry uniformly across its width.

9
Museums

Most museums which have an Egyptology collection display examples of woodwork, furniture and tools. The most important museums are listed below and visitors are advised to find out their opening times before making a special journey.

Great Britain
Ashmolean Museum of Art and Archaeology, Beaumont Street, Oxford OX1 2PH. Telephone: 0865 278000.

Birmingham Museum and Art Gallery, Chamberlain Square, Birmingham B3 3DH. Telephone: 021-235 2834.

Bolton Museum and Art Gallery, Le Mans Crescent, Bolton, Lancashire BL1 1SE. Telephone: 0204 22311 extension 2191.

Bristol City Museum and Art Gallery, Queen's Road, Bristol BS8 1RL. Telephone: 0272 223571

British Museum, Great Russell Street, London WC1B 3DG. Telephone: 071-636 1555.

Durham University Oriental Museum, Elvet Hill, Durham DH1 3TH. Telephone: 091-374 2911.

Fitzwilliam Museum, Trumpington Street, Cambridge CB2 1RB. Telephone. 0223 332900.

Glasgow Museum and Art Gallery, Kelvingrove, Glasgow G3 8AG. Telephone: 041-357 3929.

Hunterian Museum, The University of Glasgow, Glasgow G12 8QQ. Telephone: 041-330 4221.

Liverpool Museum, William Brown Street, Liverpool L3 8EN. Telephone: 051-207 0001.

Manchester Museum, The University of Manchester, Oxford Road, Manchester, M13 9PL. Telephone: 061-275 2634.

Petrie Museum of Egyptian Archaeology, University College London, Gower Street, London WC1E 6BT. Telephone: 071-387 7050 extension 2884.

Pitt Rivers Museum, University of Oxford, South Parks Road, Oxford OX1 3PP. Telephone: 0865 270927.

Royal Museum of Scotland, Chambers Street, Edinburgh EH1 1JF. Telephone: 031-225 7534.

Wellcome Museum, University College of Swansea, Singleton Park, Swansea, West Glamorgan SA2 8PP. Telephone: 0792 205678.

Austria
Kunsthistorisches Museum, Burgring 5, A-1010 Vienna.

Belgium
Musées Royaux d'Art et d'Histoire, Avenue J. F. Kennedy, 1040 Brussels.

Canada
Royal Ontario Museum, 100 Queen's Park, Toronto, Ontario M5C 2C6.

Czech Republic
Narodni Muzeum v Praze, Vitezneho Unora 74, Prague 1.

Denmark
Ny Carlsberg Glyptotek, Dantes Plads, DK-1550 Copenhagen V.

Egypt
Egyptian Antiquities Museum, Tahrir Square, Kasr el-Nil, Cairo.

France
Musée Calvet, 65 rue Joseph-Vernet, 84000 Avignon, Vaucluse.
Musée de la Vieille Charité, 2 rue de la Charité, 13002 Marseilles.
Musée des Beaux-Arts, Palais Saint-Pierre, 20 place des Terreaux, F-69001 Lyons.
Musée du Louvre, Palais du Louvre, F-75041 Paris.

Germany
Ägyptisches Museum, Staatliche Museen, Bodestrasse 1-3, 1020 Berlin.
Ägyptisches Museum, Schlossstrasse 70, 1000 Berlin 19.
Kestner-Museum, Trammplatz 3, 3000 Hanover 1.
Roemer-Pelizaeus-Museum, Amsteiner 1, 3200 Hildesheim, Niedersachsen.

Ireland
National Museum of Ireland, Kildare Street, Dublin 2.

Italy
Museo Archeologico, Via della Colonna 36, Florence.
Museo Egizio, Palazzo dell 'Accademia delle Scienze, Via Accademia delle Scienze 6, Turin.

Netherlands
Allard Pierson Museum, Oude Turfmarkt 127, Amsterdam 1012 GC.

Rijksmuseum van Oudheden, Rapenburg 28, 2311 EW, Leiden, Zuid-Holland.

Poland
Muzeum Narodowe W Krakowie, Lipcowego 12, 31-109 Krakow.
Muzeum Narodowe W Warszawie, Jerozolimskie 3, 00-495 Warszawa.

Portugal
Museu Calouste Gulbenkian, Avenide de Berna 45, 1093, Lisbon.

Russia
Pushkin Museum of Fine Arts, Volkhonka 19, 121019, Moscow.

Sweden
Medelhavsmuseet, Järntorget 84, 111 29 Stockholm.
Victoria Museum, Gustavianum, S-752 20 Uppsala.

United States of America
Brooklyn Museum, 200 Eastern Parkway, Brooklyn, New York 11238.
Field Museum of Natural History, Roosevelt Road at Lake Shore Drive, Chicago, Illinois 60605.
Metropolitan Museum of Art, Fifth Avenue at 82nd Street, New York, NY 10028.
Museum of Fine Arts, 465 Huntington Avenue, Boston, Massachusetts 02115.
Phoebe Apperson Hearst Museum of Anthropology, 103 Kroeber Hall, Berkeley, California 94720.
Rosicrucian Egyptian Museum and Art Gallery, Rosicrucian Park, San Jose, California 95191.
San Diego Museum of Man, 1350 El Prado, Balboa Park, San Diego, California 92101.
University of Chicago Oriental Institute Museum, 1155 East 58th Street, Chicago, Illinois 60637.

10
Further reading

Baines, J., and Málek, J. *Atlas of Ancient Egypt*. Phaidon, Oxford, 1980.
Baker, H. *Furniture in the Ancient World*. The Connoisseur, London, 1966.
Charlish, A. *The History of Furniture*. Orbis Books, London, 1976.
Feduchi, L. *A History of World Furniture*. Blume, Barcelona, 1977.
Garstang, J. *The Burial Customs of Ancient Egypt*. London, 1907.
Killen, G. P. *Ancient Egyptian Furniture*. Aris & Phillips, Warminster; Volume 1 1980, Volume 2 1994.
Lucas, A. *Ancient Egyptian Materials and Industries*. Editor, J. R. Harris. Arnold, London, fourth edition 1962.
Lucie-Smith, E. *Furniture: A Concise History*. Thames & Hudson, London, 1979.
Hayward, H. *World Furniture*. Hamlyn, London, 1981.
Helck, W., and Eberhard, O. *Lexikon der Agyptologie, Band IV*. Otto Harrassowitz, Wiesbaden, 1982.
Oates, P. B. *The Story of Western Furniture*. Herbert Press, London, 1981.
Petrie, W. M. F. *Arts and Crafts of Ancient Egypt*. Foulis, Edinburgh and London, 1910.
Petrie, W. M. F. *Tarkhan I and Memphis V*. British School of Archaeology in Egypt, University College London, 1913.
Petrie, W. M. F. *Tools and Weapons*. British School of Archaeology in Egypt, University College London, 1917.
Singer, C.; Holmyard E. J.; and Hall, A. R. *A History of Technology*. Clarendon Press, Oxford, 1955.

Index

Page numbers in italic refer to illustrations